LIFE in
Shades
of BLUE

Marilyn Serena Ricketts

STONE'S THROW
PUBLICATIONS

It's Complicated

The history to our history

Is a mystery not for shaking

A task worth undertaking

Eureka not for faking

To questions in the making

Who am I is this worth knowing

To keep me stagnant or help my growing

Is it ideal me that is showing?

It's a task that needs pre-empting

For each generation - no exempting

To turn a blind eye has no glory

If events unfold from ancestral stories

But no apologies if not sorry

When learnt learning doesn't last

Running backwards happens fast

And it's the future that taints the past

PUEBLO'S PICASSO AND PATCHWORK QUILT

I found
a jigsaw puzzle
of a Picasso
One or 2 pieces
were missing …
To take my mind off the crazy
I learned to quilt
with many pieces
No rhyme or reason
Method? Methodical
with patches of anything
the pieces on the quilt
Juxtaposed
like the thoughts in my head

Cry for me
Let the tears flow freely
to help wash away the pain
in time you will smile again

If I was in pain
I am now free
If I was in turmoil
I am now at rest
If I was unhappy
I am now at peace
Be easy in that ….

A book just started
is *still* just started
A letter well begun
is *still* half done
The ending only known by ONE

Be secure in the fact that you loved me
Rest assured in the fact that I loved you
We *will* see each other again, however
in the life that is to come …
This I promise you

There's a lot to be said for the power of positive thinking

and positively so, should the thinker be

But did you know….

That the unknown adversary and the watcher of the universe have taken an interest?

Regarding closely, stroking their beards – plotting new ways to mess with

the human psyche

the human resolve

the human will power

the human intention to do what is right…this time.

How to break that spirit, what up-hill battle can be concocted?

How can a cadaver, a red herring, a misnomer twist that phrase known as "the good intention"?

Their methods are the same – their intentions are not

For while the watcher knows that there is a light to the window and an open door

the unknown adversary does not want anyone to reach it

It's a game of chess but not chess – to the unknown adversary and the watcher

The human spirit is the pawn, this is true

But there's no winning- just enduring

through the negative that positive thinking can bring

How quickly will the towel be thrown in?

Will the towel be thrown in?

Be brave! Think loud! Think positive!

Be prepared to be watched.

Here's to imparted wisdom
The kind you dish out
But don't always take it-may be hard to do
Yet this is true—sometimes you have to fake it
and smile
at those who would get on your case
make you feel you're a disgrace
Welcome to the human race
Smile
and laugh
You use more muscles when you frown
Serendipity's high when it's high
and low when it's down
It's par for the course- this advice is sound
Laugh
and give
Even to those whom you would like to hate
the backstabbers, testers of your faith
Good things come to those who wait
Give
and love
all those you hold close to your heart
they are the reason you take part
in this thing called life
and life's too short
Love

ALL IN

Do you ever stop to take stock—reflecting
All the times you've laughed and cried
The friggin' emotional Barney Rubble
family roller coaster ride
Mental and physically draining arguments
Words spoken out of turn; meant then not meant
The love the hate
The hating that you love
the people you cannot hate
And so you wait and help mend the fences
Lowering defences, while those changelings
Hurt and Forgiveness yearn for their turn again
Who but the family to credit
it's to them we are indebted
Whether absent or present
Nuclear or broken—or just broken
There is no escaping the blood that binds
by blood, adoption, marriage
inclusion, dissolution, forever intertwined
Family—yours—mine
Providing the first glimmer of an answer
to the shimmer of the question
Who am I?

Madame New Year

Has 365 days but doesn't always know her age
So sometimes she leaps a few
She provides endless unknowns
and prosaic day-to-days
to make changes, remain the same
Fall in love, fall out of love
Forgive the debt, make them pay
Hold a grudge, let it go forgotten
Make promises to yourself
that you don't intend to keep
Recognize possibilities, live in the what ifs
Grow old gracefully, or die trying
Madame New Year waits for no one
and she will pass you by irrespective
of your indiscriminate mind

Square Conversations at the Round Table

Snatches of thoughts

Whispers of words

Incomplete, reverberating

Hovering just out of reach

The hanging indentations

The dangling participles

Oh how woeful not to remember!

Playing a dreadful irksome cacophonous

Game of hide and seek

Then gone! Truly gone!

Not some magician's trick

But lost in the abyss

Travelling on the sea of words

Never to return

'DECIPI FRONS PRIMA MULTOS'

(The first appearance deceives many)

"I'm filled with chagrin."
He said, while grinning
And I thought, did this blackguard
Really have a black heart?

He swaggered and swayed
With delusions of grandeur
Yet there was no alluding to illusions
Of the game being played

Infamously famous empty words
Dripping like honey
Had to laugh at the irony
Because his savvy was just….
Funny

He begged for forgiveness
With not a morsel of remorse
While trying to act like he did…
Of course

Does this dress make me look fat?

Ah the consummate mathematician!

Asks for repetition of the question

Quickly weighs the probabilities

Determining right left and middle angles

Inverting x (for dress!) and y (for fat??)

Number crunches, does the tallies

Summing up the total

Of the separate and blended outcomes

Ponders reactionary actions

Providing the best and safest answer

That which benefits him!

THROWING SHADE

You know those folks
You always knew
Could never dream in
Shades of blue
Way too flamboyant in their ways
So then why don't we throw some shade
On the colour schemes that they put paid
We watched them run amuck with green
All healthy kale and collard greens
Like all things acted out in haste
It lasted all of half a day
We saw them run around the town
'Til bright red heart turned dirty brown
And smoke grey mad – real mad tenfold!
Because we did not buy the stories sold
When steam ran out and truth be told
Their flashy silver was good as gold
But to paraphrase Maya Angelou's rhyme
"When someone shows you their colours
Believe it the *first* time"

I've given up chocolates for Lent
Friend, you don't eat chocolates (?)
That's because I've given them up for Lent

I've given up sex for Lent
Mate... you don't have a mate (?)
That's why I've given it up for Lent

I've given up smoking for Lent
But Cousin you know you don't smoke (?)
But If I did I'd have given it up for Lent

I've given up lying for Lent
Great... now I don't know what to believe (?)
God's honest! I'm telling the truth
… For Lent

JUST CHEESE NO WINE

The handsome parents
Still together
Giving off airs of aristocracy
The pretty sister
 The jock brother
Then there's me
In the shadows
Unassuming, Plain Jane
With the weight
The straight hair
With streaks of grey
Hands folded in front
Eyes cast down
Then
Wow…what're you all dressed up for?
The shoes, the slacks
Going somewhere? Who with?
Puzzled; Really? It's you he wants?
But it can't be (?)
I wonder why (?)
Then I
Burst into song

He's a super man
Not a perfect man
But the perfect man
For me
I'm the luckiest girl
In all the world
In a world filled with
All types of girls
He chose me
Wait what the fu…?!
Oh it's the stuff dreams are made of
No doubt precipitated by something I ate

A Tale of Four Sisters

Winter was temperamental. I could never really warm up to her because she always gave me the cold shoulder. I was her step sister. Had been for as long as I could remember. Their mother, Nature, was married to my father, Time. Winter and I were the same age and had gone to all the same schools. She had been in all my classes from J.K. to Uni. Fair skin, always wore white. Only those with thick skins could deal with her icy personality.

Summer was Winter's fraternal twin. She was hot. No other word for it. Everyone thought so, everyone but Winter since she and Summer never really got along. All colourful in her wardrobe and hair as golden as the sun. She was as dark as Winter was fair. Summer liked being noticed and she'd notice you only as long as you noticed her. The only problem was her attention span waxed and waned. She could never really stay in one place too long, so her relationships were never permanent.

Spring was the middle child. She loved her sisters dearly and tried hard to keep the peace between Winter and Summer. This never ended well and had her crying buckets more often than not. It made her jumpy and slightly nervous not knowing which sister to emulate. Some days she was frosty as Winter, other days she was Summer hot. Their mother kept reminding her that she should just be herself, develop her own personality. This was a work in progress.

Autumn was the baby. Just the right temperament to be loved by all her sisters and liked by those she came in contact with. She was soft spoken and genuine in her ways. She appeared to be closest to Winter, although they were three Seasons apart. Because she understood her sister's volatile ways, she would sometimes lapse into the shadows to avoid pointless confrontations. But only pointless confrontations, as she did not suffer fools gladly.

These are my sisters and this is their story.

Many a Song

'...THAT BEAUTY IS IN THE EYE OF THE BEHOLDER...'

Is phraseology suggestive
That individual perspective
Will find beauty (most subjective!)
In that which is their objective
To receive it

In the hustle and bustle of life
And living it
Words that should be said
Remain unspoken
Things that should not be said
Are said

I want you to know
That you have always
And will always be
Co-owner of my heart

Your expressions
Your emotions
Your smile
Your very physicality

Are infectious reminders
Every day new
And anew
Just how you
Simply being you
And just you
Can take my breath away

An Ode

If my life to you is like sunshine

Then your love to me is like a rose

Held dearly in its beauty and fragility

In the daylight and by moonlight; sweet repose

If being near me makes you happy

I will remain by your side

I will be your friend, lover, confidante

In this journey—together we will abide

If our friendship has no ending

And our love is not bound

And there is honesty without pretension

Over this wonderful thing we've found

A love—A marriage

Steadfast and sure

Then I am yours forever more

See you are around 10

As children we count from one to 10
Because that's easiest
There's the countdown from 10
Because that's adventure
We listen to the top 10
Because that's pop culture
10 itself is inanimate
It does not know its importance
To a decade
Evolution
Milestone
Anniversary
May the next 10 years
Find you exactly where you need to be
In the future – while the cycle repeats
See you around 10!

Love Letters to the Populace

To Friendship

How is it that I
An undeserving me
Could have a friend like you
Who could say YES!
You are deserving

How is it that I
An insignificant me
Could have a friend like you
Who could say YES!
You are important

How is it that I
An ungrateful, hateful me
Could have a friend like you
Who could say NO!
I will not judge you

The world revolves
And life evolves
The past it fades
Issues resolved
The future brings
New ones to solve
But YOU are constant

Moving On

Who said anything about goodbye?
I mean why should I even try
I have been blessed to have known you
Happy to have travelled part way on your journey
Grateful for your listening ear
Thankful for all the teardrop therapy
Pleased to know that there were other
Quirky-vintage-modern-classical-rock-jazz-opera
Binge-watching-all-things-British-people just like me
Delighted to have 'talked shop' and shopping
Fortunate that trusting few, I could trust you
Relished in your upcoming *everything*
You haven't left the earth just moved to a different space
Your *nameface* are not shadows to me
But set from an age, I think, in indelible ink
Why then would I say good-bye? I mean why should I even try
The world is round and with one thing or another
I will see you around it sometime

Dear Claude,

From you I've learned about

Green: Kale – The new lettuce; loaded with lots of stuff and that eating a kale and Nutella sandwich on white bread did not necessarily make the sandwich healthy.

Black-Brown: The Cheetah bag/jacket/shoes/bathing suit- and that cheetah wasn't cougar but more cousin to the leopard.

Blue: When you "ate your emotions" after returning from less fortunate places with a refreshed perspective.

Pink: The slight blush and a bit of frustration, when talking about the person you were trying not to talk about.

Burnt Orange: That dash of cinnamon that brought yogurt eating back in style again.

White: Nothing. Silence so pronounced from the lack of conversation and the slamming of doors, which had us wondering if we had been thinking too loudly.

Yellow: The great friend you are; bowing out gracefully so your friend could become friends with one of your friends. I STILL don't get it! However, it does say a lot about your character and what you value.

In the grand scheme of things, I wish you the very best on your
journeys and feel nothing but joy knowing you will be bringing a splash of colour to other lives, just as you've done mine.

Affectionately yours,

M

Rose – from my heart

Shakespeare said:

"What's in a name? That which we call a rose, by any other name..."

But not so! There is only one YOU

And life has decided to make some alterations

And manifest itself

In a kaleidoscope of hurdles and valleys

Leaving no choice and little option

Except to go through them

When the clouds have gone

And they WILL go

And the sun decides to shine

And it WILL shine

May you continue to be that

Same exceptional and wonderful person

Doing justice to the name you bear

"What's in a name? That which we call a rose, by any other name…"

Would not be YOU

Dear Mr. Baxter; English, Grade 9

In the Interpretive Dictionary for Teachers, volume 9

Summer Holiday is listed as:

'No more classrooms

No more books

No more children's dirty looks!'

Sleeping 'till noon

Whatever noon means to you

Walking along the beaches in the

Moonlight-sunset-your dreams

Going here—going there

Going nowhere—going wherever

On that marvelous moped of yours

Rain or shine

You earned the right to quietly chuckle

At us students who had to spend our summers

Making the grade, as you drove off with a cheery wave

Telling us all to "have a nice summer!"

Thank you so much for putting up with the invincibles

Thank you for finding something great in me

I didn't know existed

Thank you for encouraging me to always write it down

F... that! I can be anything!

I saw the perfect woman
Who looked perfect
Perfect skin
Perfect hair
Perfect figure
Everything in its place – perfectly
With the perfect men flocking around her
To worship her
She had the perfect family
With just the right amount of dysfunctionalism
To delve in the realm of perfectionism
She had the perfect friends who hung unto her
Every word – ever on the ready to defend
Her perfect honour and intelligence
Perfectly
She took the perfect selfies
Placed for the perfect people to see
On the perfect social media sites
And I knew she knew that I thought she was perfect
And she knew I knew that she thought she was perfect
That God did in fact play favourites – and all I wanted to be
Was her
But introspection took stock
 Of my own flawed self
And refused to tally
Refused to accept
Refused to conciliate
Refused to reconcile
Would not conform
To this idea
Of not being
Me
And when I woke up this morning
To my own crack'd mirror
All I wanted more than anything
Was to not be
Her

ONCE UPON A TIME...

There was a jinni in a bottle

She was her mother's daughter

A mirror image, in every way that mattered—she said

And the apple of her father's eye

Or would have been had she been a boy—he said

You're safe in your bottle and your three wishes—they said

Yet her restless spirit was not content

To be labelled by a mirror image—because that's happenstance

Or penalized for her gender—just circumstance

And she knew she may have to lose favour to gain freedom

Or there'd be missed chance

This free spirt embarked on the life long journey of SELF

Collecting along the way...

An education—SCHOOLING, INSTRUCTION, TRAINING, TEACHING

Which lead to Enlightenment—INSIGHT, UNDERSTANDING, AWARENESS, WISDOM

And gave her Purpose—AMBITION, ASPERATION, DETERMINATION

She found the Courage—BRAVERY, FORTITUDE, even AUDACITY

To Influence—LEAD, COMMAND, be ESTEEMED by her peers

Slowly forming—SHAPING, CONSTRUCTING, RE-BUILDING

Her own identity—UNIQUENESS, ONENESS, CHARACTER, and PERSONALITY

Finally; the jinni—no longer bottled by customs, norms and expectations

Developed a swagger quite avant garde—and THAT needs no explanation

THE END

**Jinni – A supernatural creature in early Arabian mythology

Life in Shades of Blue

Last night I dreamed I dreamt a dream in kaleidoscopic and restless Shades of Blue

The SAPPHIRE shone brightly so I took a leap of faith and married a slightly older CAMBRIDGE.

We lived in COLUMBIA and CAROLINA for a short while and adopted four wonderful CERULEAN children.

CORNFLOWER, CELESTE, CYAN and ETON, who were TRUE BLUE without exception.

My love for YALE and its work did not deter me from wandering for I was unsettled.

So with an AIR of SUPERIORITY I STEELED myself to join the AIR FORCE, flying BLEU DE FRANCE over sometimes DARK, occasionally DEEP, mostly MIDNIGHT, intermittently LIGHT BLUE skies.

My love for all things medieval (and CAMBRIDGE too!) saw us move lock stock TEAL barrel and BONDI children over the INTERNATIONAL KLEIN, where I worked at OXFORD, (Medieval Studies), with zeal and ZAFFRE and learned that I was ROYAL! Then CAMBRIDGE told me with a grin and twinkling IRIS, that he had been titled DUKE of PTHALO, who knew! This was however; a NON-PHOTO op and he wore DENIM to the gala.

We lived in a charming house in the country where my gardener DODGER planted excellent MAJORELLE and ELECTRIC TIFFANY in the garden the children fondly named the VIRIDIAN.

My best friends INDIGO and PERIWINKLE, who were EGYPTIAN, lived but a stone's throw away and had taught PERSIAN at UCLA.

We dressed in fashions by AZURE and FEDERAL since they were relatively unknown. MARIAN my maid had presented them at the COBALT charity banquet.

On days off when BLUE GRAY skies hinted rain, I read poetry by MAYA and wrote reflective writings.

But just like ALICE had to do, through the rabbit hole I came; finding
   that reality was not a dream but TUFTS of a dream that may one
   day be reality – CAMBRIDGE please wait for me

To dream in Shades of Blue

Marilyn Serena Ricketts has been writing poetry and short stories since being introduced to the works of author Robert Louis Stevenson, at a young age.

She was invited to recite one of her poems at the 2016 Durham Black History Month celebration. She also spoke at the Empowering Women and Young Girls event, held at the Durham Children's Aid Society.

She has won several awards for public speaking throughout her school years and has had her work published by the International Poetry Guild.

Marilyn lives in Durham Region, Ontario with her family. *Life in Shades of Blue* is her debut collection of poetry.

Manufactured by Amazon.ca
Bolton, ON

24476626R00031